Spunky Grandmas

and Other Amusing Characters

Written by Ken Mogren
Illustrated by Joella Goyette

For information, contact
MSI Press LLC
1760-F Airline Highway, #203
Hollister, CA 95023

Author: Ken Mogren
Front cover design: Joella Goyette
Book layout design: Opeyemi Ikuborije
Back cover design: Opeyemi Ikborije

ISBN: 978-1-957354-41-5

Library of Congress: 2022906038

To Sally Mogren

a spunky wife, mom, and grandma

Table of Contents

PREFACE

Today's grandmothers aren't much like their outdated stereotype. Sure, some might spend their days knitting in a rocking chair or baking pies in the kitchen, but most grandmas have much different lifestyles and far more spunk than traditionally depicted. The grandma stories in the first chapter celebrate this spunkiness.

In the chapters that follow you'll meet dozens of equally amusing characters. Each chapter has several very short stories that revolve around a theme introduced by a Joella Goyette illustration. Many of these fictional yarns were inspired by real people and events. Some are fables featuring animals acting like humans who might resemble folks you know. The final chapter, "Misfits," has tales that don't fit neatly with any of the preceding themes.

Don't be alarmed if all this looks a lot like poetry. I hesitate to use the S word (sonnet), lest it bring back painful memories of struggling in school to understand what renowned, dead poets were talking about. These are not like those. If you aren't befuddled by the poetry of Dr. Seuss and Mother Goose, you'll do just fine with these.

By the way, it's okay to enjoy these stories even if you aren't a grandma. If you like the grandma tales in the first chapter, you'll find more throughout the book whenever spunky grandma behavior lines up with a particular theme.

CHAPTER 1

Spunky Grandmas

PARKING PLACE THIEF

A grandma in a Walmart parking lot
Had driven back and forth in every aisle.
The lot was full. She couldn't find a spot,
But then a car seen leaving made her smile.

She stopped where she could easily pull in
And waited while it exited the space.
As it drove off, and much to her chagrin,
A rusty truck cut in and stole her place.

The driver when confronted smelled like booze,
And as he walked away, he turned and said,
"A lesson for you. Call it Snooze You Lose."
He later found a windshield note that read:

"A lesson for you. Call it Tit For Tat.
You'll notice all your tires now are flat."

NUISANCE PHONE CALL SOLUTION

A telemarketer was on the line.
He asked a grandma, "How are you today?"
She answered, "Well, 'til lately, things were fine,
But yesterday my husband passed away.

"It seems I've caught the virus that he had.
I've got a fever, chills, and body aches.
The diarrhea's getting pretty bad.
My head is pounding, and I've got the shakes.

"But I'm so glad you called. I feel so blue.
I'm all alone. My cat just ran away,
And I've been fretting over what to do
About some bills I can't afford to pay."

Just then she heard a click. The line went dead.
She laughed out loud. "Works every time," she said.

ROAD RAGE REVENGE

A grandma driving at a pokey pace
Enraged the driver of the car behind,
Who honked and passed like he was in a race.
Though shook a bit, she really didn't mind.

But then she saw his middle finger fly.
She thought, "He needs a lesson I should teach."
So, she sped up enough to see the guy
Turn off and park his ragtop near a beach.

And as he basked in sunshine on the sand,
With glee, she filled his flashy, top-down car
With popcorn from a beachside popcorn stand.
Soon hordes of seagulls came from near and far.

All afternoon the seagulls came and went
And splotched his car with piles of excrement.

GRANDMA GETS CARJACKED

A punk who tried to carjack Grandma's car
Demanded she get out and leave the keys.
She said, "I don't know who you think you are,
But when you ask, you could at least say please."

"Don't mess with me," the would-be car thief said.
"I've got a weapon, and I've killed before.
If you don't move, you're gonna end up dead,
And that's a warning you should not ignore."

He flashed a knife. She looked him in the eye
And said, "I don't take crap from thugs like you.
I might look old, but I'm still pretty spry,
And you should know I've got a weapon, too.

"If you were smart, you'd turn around and run.
Your knife won't stand a chance against my gun."

GRANDMA GETS FLASHED

A grandma walking in a public place
Experienced an unforeseen surprise.
A man approached. When they were face to face,
He flashed her. She could not believe her eyes.

He stood there with his coat flung open wide.
The trench coat and his shoes were all he wore.
His face displayed a look of manly pride,
A sight she couldn't easily ignore.

A moment passed, and neither made sound.
She didn't scream. Her face did not turn red.
She simply opted not to stick around,
And as she turned to walk away, she said:

"I think you'd look less silly fully dressed.
I've seen much better. I was not impressed."

APPROVAL NOT REQUIRED

Seems Grandma's clothes were getting rather tight.
When Grandpa said she ought to lose some weight,
It very nearly caused a nasty fight
For she got pleasure from the foods she ate.

She baked and ate delicious cakes and pies,
Drank wine and cappuccino every day,
Loved pizza, burgers, onion rings, and fries
And one day threw her bathroom scale away.

Time was she'd fret about what others thought.
She exercised and always was aware
Of fats and carbs in all the foods she bought.
But now she says, "I really don't much care.

"I'm happy with myself the way I am.
If folks don't like it, I don't give a damn."

CHAPTER 2

Kid Stuff

SICK AT SCHOOL

A kid who always misbehaved at school
Was very good at getting out of class.
His teacher wasn't difficult to fool
When he desired a nurse's office pass.

He'd raise his hand and say, "I'm feeling sick."
And even though this happened quite a lot,
His subterfuge would always do the trick
And land him on the nurse's office cot.

But one day when the teacher'd had enough,
She stood her ground and didn't acquiesce.
Alas, this time his claim was not a bluff.
She soon found vomit on her shoes and dress.

He asked again his absence to allow
And added, "Maybe you'll believe me now."

PLAY DATE

Two weary moms who wanted time to chat
Dispatched their children out the door to play.
Relaxed, with coffee cups in hand they sat
And hoped the kids would stay outside all day.

But soon the kids who felt a bit ignored
Were back inside to interrupt their talk.
The moms said go play hopscotch if you're bored
And handed them a box of colored chalk.

The concrete driveway made a perfect court.
With great delight, they jumped and skipped and hopped.
They got so captivated by their sport
'Twas nearly dinner time before they stopped.

Alas, the pavement had a lot of cracks
And both moms ended up with broken backs.

SCIENCE FAIR

The biggest goof-off in the seventh grade
Forgot the science fair was drawing near.
The day before, with zero progress made,
He thought, "It's time to get my butt in gear."

With no hypothesis to try to prove,
No time for research in so short a span,
He only knew that he had better move.
Then, inspiration struck. He had a plan.

He'd write eight grueling tortures on a list.
He'd do some demonstrations at his booth.
His sister's cat would be there to assist.
Experimental tests would yield the truth.

If after eight ordeals the pet survives,
He will have proven cats possess nine lives.

MEAN GIRLS

A group of six meets up each day for lunch,
Same table, same six chairs, no room for more.
Though others look for ways to join their bunch,
It's like they face a barricaded door.

Despite the vexing snobbishness they flaunt,
The clique gets watched, the envy of their peers.
They have the status other people want,
Which sometimes leaves the wannabes in tears.

Some say it's just an adolescent phase.
It starts to rear its head in middle school.
In truth, it lasts beyond our high school days.
There'll always be some groups who think they're cool.

Seems cliquishness can show up anywhere.
These gals are in a home for elder care.

CHAPTER 3

Geezers

MEMORY LOSS

An absent-minded geezer's worried wife
Had watched his mental faculties erode.
She feared it might disrupt their happy life
And searched for an effective treatment mode.

Things got no better when he exercised—
The same for mental stimulation games.
A medication she'd seen advertised
Failed horribly to validate its claims.

She looked for a support group he could try.
By chance, a group was meeting that same day.
Alas, 'twas led by some old senile guy
And morphed into a state of disarray.

Despite the chaos, no one seemed to care
For no one could recall why they were there.

TRICK OR TREAT

An old curmudgeon in the neighborhood
Was known as Mister Scrooge on Halloween.
He handed out the cheapest treats he could
And always wore a frown and acted mean.

To get his treats he never spent a dime.
Free ketchup packets from a food court bar
Were rationed out like gold, one at a time,
Which trick or treaters thought was quite bizarre.

But one kid thought, "These treats deserve some tricks."
He hacked the guy's computer in a flash,
And after just a few more well-placed clicks,
He'd maxed his credit cards and drained his cash.

Then, thanks to Fed Ex and an online store,
Scrooge found a million Kit Kats at his door.

NURSING HOME ROOSTER

The widows in a home for elder care
Perked up to see a new guy join their lot.
With all his teeth and quite a bit of hair,
Consensus was the guy was pretty hot.

It seemed to spark the ladies to compete.
The beauty parlor suddenly was filled.
A smile from him was like a special treat
That left the smitten ladies feeling thrilled.

But which of them would be the rooster's pick?
Or would he be a harem sort of guy?
His final choice made some of them feel sick,
While others shook their heads and said, "Oh, my!"

Turns out the winner, much to their dismay,
Was Ernie. Who'd have guessed they'd both be gay?

FUNERAL NO SHOW

An old guy bought the paper every day.
Obituary news was all he read.
He liked to check out who had passed away
And smiled when he was not among the dead.

He'd outlived many relatives and friends
But hated funerals, so he never went.
For this he sought a way to make amends.
So, cards of sympathy were always sent.

"I 'spose you'll skip my funeral," said his wife.
"Depends," he said. "If I'm the first to die,
I'll try to get there from the afterlife.
If you go first, I'll skip, and here is why.

"Although my logic might seem asinine,
I'll only go for folks who'll come to mine."

FREE STUFF

A man who looked for ways to save a buck
Would never pay to have things hauled away.
He'd put them on the curb. With any luck
Unwanted stuff was gone within a day:

Old furniture, appliances and tires,
stained mattresses that sat out in the rain,
Junk nobody with half brain acquires.
Why things were claimed he couldn't ascertain.

He chalked it up to people being weird
And put out even less appealing stuff.
He found that even garbage disappeared.
Recipients just couldn't get enough.

Turns out one guy was taking everything—
A cop who cited him for littering.

CHAPTER 4

A Visit to a Shrink

CRAZY HUSBAND

A lady took her husband to a shrink.
"He needs some help. I think he's nuts," she said.
"He used to love to gamble, smoke, and drink,
But now he likes to play with dolls instead."

"So, what!" The doctor said. "You should be glad.
His former habits all result in harm.
It seems to me that maybe you've gone mad.
Your husband should be sounding the alarm."

"Oh, no!" she said. "I'm not the crazy one,
And it's upsetting me to be accused.
What's crazy is his newfound form of fun.
It's shameful how he keeps himself amused.

If they were children's dolls, I wouldn't mind,
But his are all the life-size, blow-up kind."

SHE THINKS SHE'S A DOG

A man who took his wife to see a shrink
Declared, "She's nuts! You gotta help my wife.
Her dog-like ways are driving me to drink.
I'm so distraught it's ruining my life.

She chases squirrels, drinks from the commode,
And won't stop sniffing hydrants, posts, and trees.
She barks at bikes and joggers on the road
And lives in constant fear of ticks and fleas."

The doctor said, "I find hypnosis works.
It helps get goofy thinking rearranged.
I'm sure that I can rid her of her quirks.
Just tell me how you'd like to have her changed."

The husband said, "Please make her just like me.
A cat is what I'd like for her to be."

HOROSCOPE ADDICT

A lady checked her horoscope each day.
It guided her in everything she did.
She never doubted what it had to say.
If it was bad, she stayed in bed and hid.

If it was good, elation was her mood.
The world was perfect. Nothing could go wrong.
But one day later she might sit and brood
Until a better forecast came along.

Her mood swings were the cause of friends' alarm.
Bipolar mental illness was their fear.
An intervention to a funny farm
Delighted her, or so it would appear.

"My horoscope," she said, "Says it's OK.
I'm s'posed to move and meet new friends today."

MOON MAN

A quirky codger in a nursing home
Would frequently cause panic for the staff.
He had a strange propensity to roam
And moon the passing cars to get a laugh.

He'd moon the nurses, residents, and cooks.
He'd moon his roommate and his roommate's wife.
He lived to moon and see astonished looks.
Turns out he's been a mooner all his life.

A shrink was called to try to help the guy.
He mooned her, too, but afterward explained,
"I'm never good at other things I try,
But mooning is an expertise I've gained.

I get delight from entertaining folks,
And I don't care if I'm the butt of jokes."

CHAPTER 5

There's One in Every Crowd

THERE'S ONE IN EVERY CROWD

There's one in every crowd who's always late.
There's one who's vocal and who's always right.
There's one who tries in vain to lose some weight
And one who always tries to pick a fight.

There's one in every crowd who cuts the line.
There's one who's cackling laugh is much too loud.
There's one who's snobbish when it comes to wine
And one who's mad when smoking's not allowed.

There's one in every crowd who's very rude.
There's one who's on a cell phone way too much.
There's one whose jokes are always really crude
And one who's clueless, truly out of touch.

Most folks have flaws and quirks. Would you agree?
Of course, that's not the case for you and me.

LOUSY NEIGHBOR

Shall I compare him to a horse's ass?
I find my neighbor easy to despise.
He's lacking any common sense or class.
He's petty, spiteful, sneaky, and he lies.

My neighbor's yard is full of weeds and junk.
We only speak when he wants to complain.
By 10 a.m., it's likely he'll be drunk.
He's loud, obnoxious, tasteless and profane.

I get along with everyone I know.
I try to be considerate and fair.
Kind acts can make a friend of any foe,
But bounce right off this horse's derrière.

To call him such a name brings no remorse,
Except that it's an insult to a horse.

PROCRASTINATOR

Procrastination was his greatest fault
And caused a man to feel a lot of guilt.
If he could bring this problem to a halt,
He felt his hapless life might be rebuilt.

He thought, "Perhaps if I were organized,
I'd get more done. Success in life would grow.
I need to get my tasks prioritized
And rank them on a list from high to low."

He'd start on top, attack them one by one,
And scratch the finished items off each day.
He wouldn't stop until they all were done
And all his troubling guilt had gone away.

To measure progress, he'd create a chart.
He loved the plan. Tomorrow he would start.

DRAMA QUEEN

Her life was fairly normal most would say,
But she would always magnify her woes.
She swore misfortune stalked her night and day
And looked for pity when distress arose.

The slightest problem made her gripe and groan.
Life's daily tests were more than she could stand.
She couldn't bear to face them all alone.
The drama, though, was getting out of hand.

As time went by her audience declined.
Support from others happened less and less.
A sympathetic ear was hard to find
Which only made her life a bigger mess.

But still she whines, dispersing verbal spam.
She hasn't learned that no one gives a damn.

CHRONIC COMPLAINER

A man who always whined and criticized
Was never heard to utter thanks or praise.
A guy so easily antagonized
An endless stream of rants consumed his days.

He bitched about the weather, taxes, work,
Slow traffic, politicians, TV news,
His stupid boss, his neighbor who's a jerk,
And local sports teams anytime they'd lose.

But one fine day it seemed his life was charmed,
When all the things he likes to gripe about
Went perfectly. But still he was alarmed
And couldn't keep himself from freaking out.

The times for him that cause the greatest pain
Are days when there's no reason to complain.

SOCIAL MEDIA MORON

A man whose phone was never out of sight
Used Facebook, Twitter, Tik Tok, Instagram,
And though he interacted day and night,
His posts and tweets were mostly viewed as spam.

The selfies undeserving of display,
His daily photos of the stuff he ate,
And dopey tweets on issues of the day
Were either dull or apt to irritate.

Though frequently unfriended and maligned,
And though he came to be ignored by most,
And though his group of followers declined,
There was a guy who read his every post.

So, photos posted on his trip to Rome
Tipped off the guy to burglarize his home.

CHAPTER 6

Farts

THE BOY WHO FARTED IN CHURCH

'Twas just a normal Sunday morning Mass.
We sat behind a mom and two young boys
When one of them released some noxious gas,
A sneaky, wicked fart that made no noise.

The mother looked his way and rolled her eyes.
His older brother socked him on the arm.
He faked a look of innocent surprise
As if to say, "Not me? I've done no harm."

I wondered what the boy might have consumed
To manufacture gas that smelled so bad.
It reeked as though a corpse had been exhumed,
A mighty feat for such a tiny lad.

Perhaps the incident provides a clue
To why a bench in church is called a pew.

AWKWARD MOMENT

"Who farted?' was the question no one asked.
Eyes watered, and it seemed the air turned blue.
A smell incapable of being masked
Had filled the room. Folks wondered what to do.

Some looked around with smirks or rolled their eyes.
Some frowned to show that they were not amused.
The guilty party thought it would be wise
To *not* react for fear she'd be accused.

But wait! The dog was sleeping on the floor.
The awkwardness would end if he got blamed.
She grabbed his collar, marched him toward the door,
And sternly said, "You ought to be ashamed!"

But we all know the one who feels the need
To blame the dog most likely did the deed.

THE FARTIST

He had a special talent. He could fart,
Repeatedly, at will, for hours on end.
Though he considered flatulence an art,
Performances all tended to offend.

He thought his artistry might gain respect
If he could make the Guinness record book.
He found no farting records when he checked.
So, his initial act was all it took.

He set the mark for farting excellence
By asking Guinness to create a class
Called Frequent Elevator Flatulence,
His favorite venue for expelling gas.

When boasting of his triumph to his wife,
Her comment was, "You need to get a life."

LOVE STORY

A man whose wicked farts could clear a room
Was lonely, sad and yearning for a mate.
Alas, it seemed he'd never be a groom.
His courtships ended with a single date.

His farting chased potential brides away
With farts that made the paint peel off the wall.
He farts a couple hundred times a day.
He's not allowed inside the local mall.

But like the fabled beauty and the beast,
Perhaps through intervention by the gods,
And even though his farting hasn't ceased,
He's found enduring love, against all odds.

So now, at last, he's married. All is well.
He found a gal who'd lost her sense of smell.

HAUNTED HOUSE

A man tells guests, "A ghost haunts our abode,
And though it doesn't visually appear,
Whenever there's a haunting episode,
It makes distinctive noises you can hear.

At times, you'll hear a cluck, a click, or clack
And other times a chirp, a squawk, or squeak.
It might be like a pop, a croak, or quack
Or air escaping from an unseen leak.

And you can also tell the ghost's nearby
If you detect a yucky, putrid smell."
But frequent guests have figured out the guy
And don't believe the tale he likes to tell.

It's just a fabrication by the host
So he can fart and say that it's the ghost.

CHAPTER 7

Quirky Women

ALWAYS LATE

Delivered by her mother three weeks late,
It set the tone for all the years ahead.
Her tardiness was her defining trait,
A reputation she would never shed.

Her friends and colleagues hated her delays.
She never came on time to an event.
She held up meetings, parties, holidays,
Was late for work and late to pay the rent.

In time, like most, with age her health grew bad.
A doctor said the end of life was nigh.
Though days or weeks were all he thought she had,
She lived two years and thus was late to die.

Her funeral Mass was set for half past eight.
Friends came at nine. They knew that she'd be late.

DISNEY FANATIC

A lifelong Disney fan was nearing death
But woke up all excited from a dream,
Inspired to act before her final breath
To plan her funeral with a Disney theme.

The mortuary people took great pains
To work the plan so nothing would go wrong.
The seven dwarfs would carry her remains,
And Ariel would sing a funeral song.

Then, just before they closed the casket lid,
A handsome prince would give a final kiss.
She hoped to waken just like Snow White did.
They'd marry and enjoy eternal bliss.

So, as he bent to kiss, excitement surged.
Alas, when he was done, a frog emerged.

LOTTERY WINNER

She'd hoped the lottery would change her life
And bought a ticket nearly every week
But saw no end to economic strife.
Then, all that changed, and she could hardly speak.

A hundred million dollars was the prize.
The numbers matched the ticket in her purse.
She thought at first, "I can't believe my eyes.
I hope that sudden wealth is not a curse."

She couldn't sleep. Her life would be so great.
She planned all night just how she'd spend the dough.
But then she noticed that the ticket's date
Was from the game she'd played two weeks ago.

She still buys tickets. Hopes to win some day,
But now she throws the losing ones away.

SUPERSTITIOUS LADY

A man who had a superstitious wife
Had watched her strange behaviors through the years.
He thought, "It's time that I improve her life,"
And set out to disprove her silly fears.

'Twas Friday on the thirteenth of July,
He smashed a mirror much to her alarm.
His walk beneath a ladder made her sigh.
She gasped as he destroyed her lucky charm.

He opened three umbrellas in the room
And then allowed black cats to cross his path.
Despite these acts inviting certain doom,
The Gods of Superstition showed no wrath.

.

"You see," he said, "You need not fear bad luck."
The next day he was flattened by a truck.

KARAOKE QUEEN

She yearned to be a karaoke star.
Each week on Friday night at nine o'clock,
She'd step onstage inside a local bar
And sing some classic show tunes, blues, or rock.

Regardless of the genre of her choice,
A bunch walked out; some booed, and some threw beer.
Alas, she had a truly dreadful voice,
And that's what caused the hostile atmosphere.

It seemed success required something new.
She thought about adjustments to her act,
And then she figured out what she should do.
So, now when she performs, the place is packed.

And though they plug their ears, their eyes are glued
Since she began performing in the nude.

CHAPTER 8

Animals Who Drink

RUNNING FROM BEARS

A drunken bear who'd just devoured a man
Was bragging to his buddies in a bar.
"Some hikers saw me, so they turned and ran
And tried to get to where they'd parked their car.

Each knew he wasn't faster than a bear
But thought if he could outrun just one friend,
I'd catch the slow guy, stop, and dine right there.
At least, that's how they thought it all would end.

They didn't know that worn-out myth's not true.
To outrun friends is really a mistake.
I think the truly sporting thing to do
Is chase the swift and give the slow a break."

"Besides," he said, "I'm sure you'd all attest
The fastest runners always taste the best."

SLOW AND SLOWER

A sloth and snail were talking in a bar,
Bemoaning life's incessant hectic pace.
The sloth said, "Things have gone a bit too far.
It feels as if I'm in a constant race."

"Me too and I'm the slowest," said the snail.
"Life never seemed this crazy in the past.
Today's world values speed, and slowpokes fail.
Too bad we're not like cheetahs. We'd be fast."

The barmaid couldn't help but overhear
And said, "I doubt that I can solve your plight,
But I've got some advice about your beer.
You haven't made much progress yet tonight.

You'd best drink up or you won't finish them.
It's ten o'clock. We close at two AM."

GLOOMY LAB RATS

Two lab rats in a bar one Friday night
Recounted horrors of the prior week.
One said, "They gave me some new lymphocyte,
And now it hurts like hell to take a leak."

"That's nothing," said the other. "See this burn?
They put me in a complicated maze.
Electro shocks from each improper turn
Produced this wound. I haven't slept in days."

Just then a third rat stepped up to the bar,
A smiling, upbeat, healthy-looking guy.
Although his cheerful manner seemed bizarre,
They'd seen his type before, so they knew why.

They both got up and moved from where they'd sat
To not be near the smug, control group rat.

GROUNDHOG DAY

Two groundhog guys, half snockered in a bar,
Had been discussing Punxsutawney Phil.
They didn't like their species' biggest star
And questioned his prognosticating skill.

"Both you or I could do as well," said one.
"He's wrong at least as often as he's right.
There's no way one day's view of clouds or sun
Can peg the date that Spring will be in sight."

"Darn right!" the other said, "And what I hate
Is how he struts and poses for the press
And how those guys in top hats think he's great,
But maybe I'm just jealous, I confess.

He's such a jerk and damned if I know why
So many groundhog women love the guy."

TOO DRUNK TO DRIVE

A drunk raccoon about to leave a bar
Was halted by his friend, a sober skunk,
Who said, "You really shouldn't drive your car.
I'll take you home tonight. You're way too drunk."

"That's nonsense," slurred the much-annoyed raccoon.
"I haven't had that much, and I feel fine"
The skunk said, "No, you've been in here since noon.
To think you're fit to drive is asinine."

"OK, I'll walk," replied the drunk raccoon.
"I live just down the road. It's not too far."
He staggered out the door and very soon
Was struck and splattered by a passing car.

So, now when you see roadkill as you drive,
You'll know just why those creatures aren't alive.

TRASH TALKING ANIMALS

A moose and bear were chatting in a bar,
Exchanging boasts and insults as they talked.
The moose said, "Hunters come from near and far.
You can't believe how often I get stalked."

"I'm sure they'd like your antlers," said the bear,
"But far more hunters prize a bearskin rug."
Annoyed, the moose looked over with a glare
And said "You bears excel at being smug.

We sleep outside all winter 'cuz we're tough.
You wussy bears hole up and hibernate."
The bear said, "I suppose it's pretty rough
To face the fact you creatures aren't as great.

Your species feels inferior, I'd guess
Because your plural doesn't end in S."

CHAPTER 9

Crabby Old Ladies

BUSYBODY NEIGHBOR

She seemed to buy a lot of things online.
A FedEx truck was often at her house.
Her nosy neighbor thought she'd seen a sign
The lady might be cheating on her spouse.

While normal FedEx stops are very quick,
His half-hour inside visits were routine.
The neighbor thought, "This really makes me sick.
I've got to tell her husband what I've seen."

She told him, "I'm not one to dredge up smut,
And what I've got to say might make you sad,
But you deserve to know your wife's a slut."
To her surprise, he wasn't even mad.

"You see," he said. "You're wrong about your hunch.
They're siblings, and he sometimes stops for lunch."

NO FILTER

She lacks a filter twixt her mouth and brain
And says whatever might be on her mind.
Oblivious to causing others pain,
Her vitriol is more than just unkind.

She's unaware of being seen as rude.
She'll criticize her relatives and friends
With words indelicate and often crude,
For which she never tries to make amends.

In younger days, she wasn't near as blunt.
In situations where she'd interact,
Great care was taken never to affront
And handle things with deference and tact.

It's common that as some advance in years,
The filtering of comments disappears.

GOLF WIDOW

A golfer's foursome now is down to three.
They'd played together almost every day
'Til sadly, one day on the seventh tee,
He had a heart attack and passed away.

The members of his club showed up in force
To spread his ashes on a long par five.
Eternal rest would happen on the course
He'd loved and played so often while alive.

The perfect send-off thought his golfing friends,
But absent from the tribute was his wife.
She'd always hoped he'd someday make amends
For making golf the center of his life.

"I doubt I'll miss him," she was heard to say.
"I hardly ever saw him anyway."

HOARD OF PLENTY

A lady never threw a thing away.
Her house was jammed with stuff from wall to wall.
Her oldest son confronted her one day
And told her, "When you die, we'll toss it all.

"Accumulating stuff is a disease.
Support groups are a way to help you quit."
Reluctantly and only to appease,
She found a group and got involved with it.

They'd meet beside a dumpster once a week.
Each had to bring a dozen things to toss.
'Twas meant to be a curative technique,
But purging brought a grievous sense of loss.

So, she'd return to take back what she'd thrown,
Plus other stuff she now is glad to own.

CHAPTER 10

Rednecks

DISCO DISDAIN

Two rednecks in a bar one afternoon
Were drinking shots and beers and swapping lies
When someone played a jukebox disco tune,
A music genre rednecks all despise.

It quickly sparked a nasty barroom brawl.
The disco fan was booted out the door.
Seems rednecks, when they're fueled by alcohol,
Find irritants aren't easy to ignore.

The cops were called. The rednecks went to jail.
In cuffs and jumpsuits, they appeared in court.
They'd hoped the judge would let them out on bail
And sweated while he read the cops' report.

The judge said, "I'm appalled by disco, too.
You're free to go. I'm proud of both of you."

REDNECK YARD DECOR

His yard gets praised by all his redneck friends.
It has that just right tackiness appeal,
A not-so-chic display of odds and ends
That radiates a cluttered, trashy feel.

The look did not require a lot of bucks.
Old plumbing fixtures peeking through the weeds,
A stove, an old TV, some junked out trucks,
The souvenirs of life a great yard needs.

He knows that most who see it won't applaud.
They view it as a junkyard full of waste.
His joy is knowing rednecks will be awed
For they possess a keener sense of taste.

And to those neighbors who do not approve,
He says, "If you don't like it, you can move."

REDNECK NEIGHBORS

She asked a psychic, "Would you please advise?
A redneck clan has moved in right next door.
Our neighborhood was once a paradise,
But they behave in ways that I deplore.

They sleep all day, then drink and yell all night.
Their dogs and chickens poop on my front lawn.
When I complain, they raise their fists to fight.
I don't know what to do. I want them gone."

The psychic answered, "Ouch! I feel your pain.
They seem disgusting, brazen, crass and crude.
Like you, I view your neighbors with disdain,
But honestly, I'd have to say you're screwed.

The only way you'll see your life improve
Is buy insurance, burn your house, and move."

REDNECK BUCKET LIST

Ol' Jim Bob got ticked off and punched his boss.
Of course, this quickly led to being fired.
He thought, " This crappy job ain't no big loss.
I'll make a bucket list. I'm now retired.

I'll drink more beer and take a brewing class.
I'll patch up all the rust spots on my truck.
I've now got time to poach some lunker bass
And maybe even shine a trophy buck.

I think I'll start a beard and never shave,
The gals will think I'm sexier, I'll bet.
I hope to pee on my old boss's grave.
I want to die a million bucks in debt.

I'll plan my funeral. It will be deluxe.
I'll meet St. Peter in a camo tux."

REDNECK HOLIDAY HOSTING TIPS

When hosting rednecks for the holidays,
Beware of bad mistakes you must avoid.
A brawl touched off by just a word or phrase
Will surely cause some stuff to be destroyed.

Don't talk about which brand of truck is best.
Don't ask your guests to go outside to smoke.
Don't mention NASCAR drivers you detest.
Don't scold a child who tells a raunchy joke.

Besides the don'ts, remember all the dos.
Allow the guests to park in your front yard.
Buy lots of beer, but water down the booze.
Expect disputes. Preventing them is hard.

And pray that if an argument persists,
It's settled without bullets, merely fists.

CHAPTER 11

Quirky Men

IMAGINARY FRIEND

A boy who spent a lot of time alone
Created an imaginary friend,
And even when the lad was fully grown,
The long-established friendship didn't end.

They sometimes went on road trips in his car.
They liked to go to movies of all sorts,
And often they would hang out in a bar
Where they'd get stinking drunk while watching sports.

'Twas almost certain they'd be friends for life.
Alas, their closeness sparked some jealousy.
He got an ultimatum from his wife,
"You'll have to choose," she said. "It's him or me."

Ignoring her was what he chose to do
For she was just imaginary, too.

ONLINE IMPOSTOR

He placed his profile on a dating site.
Attracting lovely ladies was his plan.
He knew exaggeration wasn't right,
But goddesses expect a perfect man.

He lied about his past, his job, his car.
He lied about his talents, age, and height.
He used a picture of a movie star.
It wasn't long before he had a bite.

Her message read, "At last! My kind of guy."
Her photo and her profile made him drool.
They met. Alas, she too was prone to lie,
So both were duped, and each felt like a fool.

Yet, strangely somehow love began that night,
Which proves two wrongs can sometimes make a right.

MAN IN PINK

A quirky man would always dress in pink—
Pink shirts, pink pants, pink socks and underwear.
When he got dressed, he never had to think
For pink stuff was the only clothing there.

His wardrobe led to rumors and some jokes.
A kinky fetish? Some strange fantasy?
But such were faulty theories by those folks
For things were not what they appeared to be.

His color preference always had been white.
But when he got divorced and lived alone,
The laundry chores he sought to expedite
Were bungled, thanks to things he'd never known.

He didn't know that fabric colors bled,
And all his towels just happened to be red.

COMPULSIVE PHOTOGRAPHER

He never really saw the sights of Rome.
He always had his camera in the way.
He figured he could wait 'til he got home
And live his travels on some future day.

He photo'd every aspect of his trip:
Cathedrals, paintings, pigeons in a square,
The food he ate, his stateroom on the ship,
The statues of DaVinci and Voltaire.

But just before his journey was complete,
Through carelessness and momentary haste,
Regrettably, he somehow pressed delete,
And all his photos instantly erased.

Without those pictures of the things he'd done,
He'll never ever know if he had fun.

SING-ALONG GUY

A fan of nearly any type of song
Enjoyed the streaming music in his car.
Alas, he always liked to sing along
And thought he was a vocal superstar.

His high opinion of his voice was sad.
Off-key and raspy, always much too loud,
With butchered lyrics, he was truly bad
And should have felt ashamed, yet he was proud.

'Twas fine when he was driving all alone,
But passengers were very much annoyed.
His wife would always plug her ears and groan.
Their marriage sadly almost was destroyed.

But now if they must travel very far,
Alone, she drives the couple's other car.

CHAPTER 12

A Toast to Healthy Living

DOCTOR'S ORDERS

A doctor gave his patients good advice.
To smokers, it was, "Toss those cigarettes!"
To those who drank, he warned, "You'll pay a price!"
He guaranteed they'd later have regrets.

He never hesitated to advise
That heavy patients ought to lose some weight.
He preached that healthy foods and exercise
Would keep them looking fit and feeling great.

But wellness was for others, not for him.
He lived on junk food, drank too much, and smoked.
He never saw the inside of a gym
And wasn't even fifty when he croaked.

Seems expertise alone is not enough.
Smart people sometimes do the dumbest stuff.

HYPOCHONDRIAC

A man who when he read or watched TV,
Was mesmerized by news about disease.
He often thought, "Those symptoms sound like me,"
Which always left him feeling ill at ease.

He swore he had a tumor in his brain.
His pancreas was cancerous he feared.
His wife was sick of hearing him complain
And wondered how she'd wed a man so weird.

Although he truly thought that he was ill,
His doc said, "You're a hypochondriac.
I can't prescribe a treatment or a pill.
You need a shrink. Please go, and don't come back."

The next day he collapsed, and death came quick.
His tombstone reads, "I told you I was sick."

WEIGHT LOSS EXPERT

"I lost a hundred twenty pounds," she said.
"That's why I chose to write a diet book.
It's good advice for folks with pounds to shed.
They're gonna love the way they feel and look."

She claimed that when her weight loss quest began,
She pledged to eat no ice cream for a year.
She'd stick to fibrous foods like beans and bran
And stop consuming soft drinks, wine, and beer.

But how she tracked the weight she claimed she dropped
Was one of many things that weren't explained,
Like weight-maintaining habits to adopt
Or all the pounds that she herself regained.

Turns out her feat was smaller than it sounds.
A dozen times she'd lost the same ten pounds.

HEALTHY FOOD SNOB

A lady who seemed fussy when she ate
Told friends that healthy foods were all she'd touch.
She preached, "Organic vegetables are great.
I'll eat some grass-fed beef but not too much."

She talked about the foods she never chose.
She scoffed at trans fats, blasted pesticides,
Had little time for any GMOs,
And knew what nutrients each food provides.

But when alone with no one to impress,
Her dietary habits were obscene.
She snacked on chips and cookies to excess
And mostly dined on fast food junk cuisine.

When fadsters climb aboard the latest trend,
Their dedication might be just pretend.

CHAPTER 13

Another Day at Work

SICK DAY

Her health seemed free of abnormalities,
Yet she was prone to call in sick a lot.
Her frequent cold and flu type maladies
Made bosses wonder, " Is she sick or not?"

One sick day at the food court in a mall,
Heroically, she saved a choking child.
A nearby cell phone camera caught it all,
And soon the news and Internet went wild.

But busted, playing hooky got her fired,
A P.R. goof that got her boss fired, too.
An offer came for her to be rehired,
But she declined and bid her job adieu.

Some sudden wealth had lifted her despair.
The toddler's grandma was a billionaire.

OCCUPATIONAL HAZARD FOR A MIME

A street-performing mime had done his show.
'Twas time to take a break and have some lunch.
From food he'd packed for eating on the go,
He grabbed a sandwich, then began to munch.

Alas, it seems he took too big a bite.
Some food got stuck, and he began to choke.
His face displayed a chilling look of fright.
He struggled like a man about to croak.

A choking man should cause folks to react.
Though many might have helped him, no one tried.
They thought it was an encore to his act.
So, dozens stood there watching as he died.

Asphyxia was ruled to be the cause,
But he passed on to thunderous applause.

BRING YOUR PET TO WORK DAY

A boss who sought a way to boost morale
Declared that pets could now be brought to work
And any pet could come. His rationale
Was all employees ought to have this perk.

He hadn't thought of problems this might cause
Until the odor from a skunk began.
He learned respect for alligator jaws
And watched a python try to crush a man.

His customers were having to beware,
And this was causing him to have regrets.
The day had made him painfully aware
How weird his workers are to own such pets.

So, now the rules are like they were before.
It's once again a pet free Walmart store.

OFFICE BUTT KISSER

He got a raise despite a budget cut.
'Twas dumb to brag about it to his peers.
They'd all seen how he kissed the boss's butt—
A vile way, most think, to boost careers.

The boss was both a doofus and a jerk,
Unworthy of the suck-up's lavish praise.
So, Mister Buttkiss had no friends at work,
And colleagues cheered when he saw darker days.

He knew he'd had it when the boss got canned.
His most disturbing nightmare had come true.
A guy who loathed him now was in command,
So, Buttkiss very soon got booted too.

The lesson that he learned from all of this:
Be careful when you choose whose butt to kiss.

JOB SECURITY

The fastest typist in the steno pool
Had skills that would be classified "elite."
She lost her job. It seemed unjust and cruel,
But changing times had made her obsolete.

She found employment in a photo store.
She'd print your pictures in an hour or less.
But digital pushed Kodak out the door,
And progress once again made life a mess.

She looked for work more stable than she'd had,
A job that innovation can't erase.
Alas, the next one also turned out bad
When streaming killed her movie rental place.

But now she's a barista, worry free,
'Cuz coffee snobs mean job security.

MORTUARY MIRTH

An undertaker who was once a clown
Thought funeral customs needed to be changed.
The somber mood left people feeling down.
'Twas not the case at funerals he arranged.

He wore a yellow tux. His hearse was pink.
An open bar served cocktails, beer, and wine,
And after mourners had a bit to drink,
He had them join him in a conga line.

A juggler and a mime amused the crowd.
His greatest joy was entertaining folks.
While eulogists and clergy were allowed,
He told them, "Keep it short, and tell some jokes."

To put the fun in funeral was his aim.
"A funeral that's to die for" was his claim.

ATTORNEY ETHICS

A senile senior in declining health
Retained a lawyer who prepared a will.
Because the gent possessed a lot of wealth,
The lawyer sent him quite a hefty bill.

He tripled what would be his normal rate.
The geezer was in no shape to complain.
Besides, the bill was dwarfed by his estate.
The lawyer's calloused conscience felt no pain.

But soon he faced a sticky, moral plight.
The client's check had caused a double take.
The guy had paid him ten times what was right,
An extra zero written by mistake.

He agonized, then opted not to dare
To tell his partners, lest they'd want to share.

CHAPTER 14

Creepy Guys

FIRST-TIME FLASHER

He bought a trench coat off the bargain rack.
A first-time flasher has to look the part.
He saved the tags so he could take it back
In case he later had a change of heart.

He thought he'd like to flash a gorgeous blonde.
He took great pride in what he had to show.
He fantasized about how she'd respond.
It wouldn't take too long before he'd know.

He saw the perfect woman on the street.
His heart was beating at a frantic pace.
He circled 'round in order that they'd meet,
Then flashed her when positioned face-to-face.

She pointed as she laughed. He slinked away.
He'd flash no more. The coat went back that day.

INFLATABLE GIRLFRIEND

He wasn't thought of as a ladies' man.
He'd always been a shy and awkward guy.
If men can't get a girl, their money can
When she's a blow-up doll that they can buy.

His friends would see her riding in his car.
When asked about it, he would just explain
That she could pass for human from afar
And with her he could use the carpool lane.

But there were secret things he didn't tell.
He bought her sexy clothes and lingerie
Until his world became a living hell
The day she dumped him, much to his dismay.

When she explained, he took it very hard.
She'd met the blow-up Santa in his yard.

COUGAR BAIT

He never had much luck with girls his age.
With younger girls he never got too far,
Then this advice came from a trusted sage,
"Sing karaoke in a cougar bar.

"You're no Sinatra, but your voice ain't bad;
They'll scratch each other's eyes out over you.
'The Girl From Ipanema' drives them mad,
And any song by Barry White will, too."

He soon became a karaoke hit
And had his choice of cougars every night.
'Twas fun at first but he grew tired of it
When one night lust affairs stopped feeling right.

The incident that caused the thrill to fade
Was sleeping with his teacher from third grade.

PICK-UP LINE

A creepy guy was sitting in a bar
And saw a gorgeous babe across the room.
The perfect pick-up line might take him far,
And love or lust, at least, would be abloom.

He sauntered over, winked at her, and smiled,
Then said " I think I know you from somewhere,"
A line he hoped might render her beguiled
And conversation would take off from there.

She didn't speak, just looked him in the eye.
He stood there with a mix of hope and dread
And anxiously awaited her reply,
Then slinked away, deflated, when she said,

"If you and I had met somewhere before,
I'd surely never go there anymore."

CRADLE ROBBER

A senior took a freshman to the prom.
"I like 'em young" is what he told his friends.
In nine months, she became a teenage mom,
But that's not where his creepy story ends.

His fondness never waned for youthful gals.
He married often, always young, of course.
He loved to show them off to jealous pals,
But gaining weight or wrinkles meant divorce.

Except for wealth, the guy was no great prize,
But riches help offset a lot of flaws
For ladies drawn to wealthy older guys
Who want to get his money in their paws.

So, when he robbed the cradle one last time,
His bimbo widow snatched up every dime.

CLOSING-TIME CASANOVA

At ten o'clock, he looked around the bar
And saw a gal he rated as a three.
"No way," he thought. "She's just not up to par.
I'd like at least a nine. She's not for me."

When midnight came, he'd had a lot to drink.
His quest for lust was into overdrive.
The alcohol had caused him to rethink,
And now he'd upped her rating to a five.

Although he hoped he still might meet a nine,
Each sip made her attractiveness improve.
As closing time approached, she looked just fine.
So, right before last call, he made his move.

And when he took her home, she was a ten.
Alas, by morn, she'd dropped to three again.

WEDDING PARTY HOOK-UP

He ushered at the wedding of a pal
And met a bridesmaid who had turned his head,
A stunning, single goddess of a gal.
His goal became to get her into bed.

She didn't want a drink or care to dance.
She seemed content to simply sit and talk.
That didn't seem the fast track to romance.
So, he suggested they might take a walk.

"OK, she said, "It's pretty loud in here."
They strolled together down a quiet path.
He took her hand, then saw a look of fear,
And in her voice he heard a tone of wrath.

"Enough," she said, "That's not my kind of fun.
I guess nobody told you I'm a nun."

CHAPTER 15

Vanity

BAD PLASTIC SURGERY

The mirror told an aging gal the truth,
"You're like a faded flower, fair no more."
She'd seen an ad that promised long-lost youth
A plastic surgeon's work could help restore.

She met the doc, who said, "You'll be a ten!
A boob job, butt lift, plus a tummy tuck
Will have your body looking young again,
And I've got time this week, so you're in luck!"

He also used some Botox on her face,
enlarged her lips, and redesigned her nose.
Alas, the surgeon's skills were a disgrace.
She looked as if she'd melted, then refroze.

So, now the ill effects of vanity
Are there as evidence for all to see.

COMBOVER GUY

A narcissistic man was losing hair
And thought he ought to camouflage his plight.
He didn't want his friends to be aware
Lest they might tease him if it came to light.

A hair growth product proved to be a scam.
He couldn't find a suitable toupee.
Though combovers are blatantly a sham,
He made it his solution anyway.

The snickering of others went unheard.
He failed to notice all the stares and smirks.
Seems some folks' image of themselves gets blurred
And blinds them to awareness of their quirks.

And so attempts to hide his balding dome
Went on 'til there was nothing left to comb.

TATTOO REMORSE

A former lover's name inside a heart,
Some lyrics from a song you now despise,
The skull you thought to be a work of art—
Tattoos you got that proved to be unwise.

Was it just impulse? Pressure from your peers?
It could have been rebelliousness, of course.
Or maybe you just drank too many beers,
And now you've got tattoos that bring remorse.

But if you think that life would be improved,
A laser treatment you can now obtain
Can get unwanted old tattoos removed
Though you'll incur a lot of cost and pain.

But if you do, you ought to keep just one
To help remind of foolish things you've done.

BALD GUY HAIRCUT

A bald guy asked his barber for a trim
Despite the fact he didn't have much hair.
The barber quickly went to work on him,
And soon the man was looking debonair.

The job was done, and it was time to pay.
The bald guy told him, "You should charge me less.
If you could work on guys like me all day,
You'd be a multi-millionaire, I'd guess."

The barber stood his ground and said, "You're wrong.
If you had timed me, there'd be no debate.
A bald guy hair cut takes me just as long,
But nonetheless, I charge a different rate.

"The clipping and the snipping all come free,
But bald guys are assessed a finder's fee."

CHAPTER 16

Come Fly with Me

EMOTIONAL SUPPORT ANIMALS

When pets who give emotional support
Became prohibited on airline flights,
One man declared, "I'll challenge this in court.
My goat and I must stand up for our rights."

He told the judge, "I'm terrified to fly.
Without my goat nearby to calm my fears,
I go berserk and think I'm gonna die.
Seems crazy, but I've been this way for years.

"Besides," he said, "my job depends on this
Cuz travel is a must for my career."
The judge said, "Well, I guess I'd be remiss
To rule against what seems a valid fear."

So, he still brings the goat that keeps him sane.
That's good cuz he's the pilot of the plane.

WHEN PIGS FLY

I looked up from my aisle seat, 14C,
And saw a huge man step aboard the plane.
I thought let's hope he's not in 14B,
If so, this flight will surely be a pain.

He waddled down the aisle and stopped by me.
I closed my eyes and said a silent prayer.
Next thing I knew he tapped me on the knee
And said, " Hey pal, I think my seat's right there."

Not only did his sprawl invade my space,
His body odor couldn't be ignored.
He wheezed and sneezed and coughed right in my face,
He sweated, farted, belched, then slept and snored.

I wish those choose-your-seat maps let me see
The person who'd be sitting next to me.

CONVERSATION ON A PLANE

A redneck and a wine snob on a plane
Sat side by side, each thirsty for a drink.
The wine snob said, "I'll have your best champagne."
The redneck said, "I'll try that, too, I think."

The wine snob swirled his glass and took a sip.
The redneck gulped his down with one big chug.
The wine snob said, "I'll offer you a tip.
This isn't beer. That's not a frosty mug."

Revenge for that remark seemed apropos.
The redneck knew exactly what to do.
"Of wine," he said, "There's much that I don't know,
But I'm a snuff snob. Here's a tip for you:

Tobacco juice makes everything taste fine.
Here, I'll just spit a little in your wine."

AIRWHINES

As airlines merge and competition fades,
Their prices rise, and comforts disappear.
Though passengers give falling, failing grades,
The airlines' attitudes seem cavalier.

They steal our legroom as they add more seats.
We miss connections 'cuz of their delays.
They're stingier with beverages and treats.
Our luggage sometimes disappears for days.

But they don't care for they are in control.
Competitors mistreat their patrons, too.
Their bottom line is now the only goal.
There's little angry passengers can do.

And with new fees for things that once were free,
It won't be long until we pay to pee.

CHAPTER 17

Happy Holidays

THE REAL RUDOLPH

The North Pole reindeer stable was abuzz.
'Twas time to harness up to pull the sleigh,
But no one seemed to know where Rudolph was,
Last seen inside a bar the prior day.

He'd gone on benders many times before,
Tried rehab twice, alas to no avail.
With bloodshot eyes, he staggered through the door.
He'd gotten drunk and spent the night in jail.

When Santa saw him, he just shook his head.
"That's it!" he said, "You're grounded for tonight."
With Dasher flying in the lead instead,
They registered their fastest-ever flight.

It's not well known and almost never said,
But booze explains why Rudolph's nose is red.

COUNTING BLESSINGS

A spotted owl and wolf were in a bar,
Half drunk, the night before Thanksgiving Day.
Each sipped fine wine and smoked a big cigar
And talked of blessings that had come their way.

"I'm thankful I'm endangered," said the owl.
"The law protects me, so I can't be harmed."
"I'm blessed with talent," said the wolf. "I howl.
Though it's entrancing, some folks get alarmed."

The owl replied, "It's not the sound you make.
Your predatory ways are what they fear.
Your status as protected is at stake.
We're apt to see your species disappear."

The wolf just grinned and said, "I think you're right,"
Then ate the owl in just a single bite.

REGIFTING

A lady got a really ugly gift,
A statue of a pig in a beret.
'Twas big and bulky, difficult to lift.
She thought, "I've got to give this thing away."

She gave it to a niece she didn't like,
Who gave it to a cousin she despised,
Who gave it to her neighbor's little tyke,
Whose mom was most unpleasantly surprised.

A sister of the mom was next in line.
She opened it, got mad, and nearly cursed,
Then thought, "'Tis better to regift than whine,"
And gave it to the gal who'd had it first.

A lousy gift should just be thrown away.
You pass it on, it might come back some day.

REDNECK GRANDMA'S CHRISTMAS LETTER

First, Junior wrecked his truck on New Year's Day.
Then, Billy Bob got busted shining deer,
And then when Walmart fired Lulu Mae,
We figured this ain't gonna be our year.

In June, I joined a brawl outside a bar.
I lost a tooth, so now I'm down to three.
Our coon dog got run over by a car.
Our trailer's porch got flattened by a tree.

We still don't know who knocked up Thelma Jo.
It could have been at least a dozen guys.
It might have been her dad for all we know
'Cuz little Bubba seems to have his eyes.

Although it's been a pretty lousy year,
From all of us we send you Christmas cheer.

TURKEY TALK

Two turkeys drinking beer were in a bar,
Half-drunk the night before Thanksgiving Day.
One said, "We're smarter than our peers by far.
We dodged their fate the night we ran away."

The other bird said, "I propose a toast.
To us! The smartest turkeys in the pen.
Tomorrow while our former comrades roast,
We'll sober up and then get drunk again."

The barmaid smiled and said, "This one's on me."
She filled their mugs, then brought them several more.
Delighted to be getting drunk for free,
They very soon were passed out on the floor.

The barmaid grabbed an axe and honed the blade.
Beer proved to be a tasty marinade.

CHAPTER 18

Busted. Tell It to the Judge

GRAFFITI ARTIST

The courthouse brick and stone had just been cleaned,
A perfect canvas for graffiti paint
Until the local sheriff intervened
And had to force himself to use restraint.

"Put down the paint, and stick 'em up," he said.
The artist tried to run to no avail.
He'd only gone a block from where he'd fled
When he was captured, cuffed, and sent to jail.

He held out hope the judge might understand.
Perhaps he'd value creativity
And recognize an artist's skillful hand.
The judge's comments proved 'twas not to be.

He said, "A month in jail will make you smart.
You'll learn that vandalism isn't art."

CELLPHONE VIGILANTE

Loud cellphone talking in a public place
Can make those forced to hear it feel annoyed.
A grandma thought, "Those jerks are a disgrace,"
And vowed to see their cellphones all destroyed.

She'd go to public places, hang around,
And spot offenders; then, to their surprise,
She'd snatch their cellphones, slam them to the ground,
And stomp on them before their very eyes.

Surveillance footage landed her in jail.
But when the prosecutor told the court,
"This menace shouldn't be released on bail."
The judge responded with this quick retort:

"I hear those morons, too, and I get pissed.
She ought to get a medal. Case dismissed!"

ROAD RAGE

The other driver made his temper flare.
He'd cut him off and forced him to slow down.
He passed the jerk, looked over with a glare,
And thought, "I'll now get even with this clown."

He got in front and slowed to just a crawl.
The other driver scowled as he passed back.
Incensed by this audacious show of gall,
The road-raged driver planned his next attack.

He waited 'til they reached the next red light,
Then stepped out and approached the other car.
He shook his fist and yelled "C'mon, let's fight!"
The confrontation never got that far.

A zapping from a taser made him stop
His taunting of the undercover cop.

JOINT CUSTODY

A bad decision made with little thought,
A marriage that went badly from the start.
Attempts to patch things up had gone for naught,
So, both agreed that it was time to part.

Each walked away with minimal remorse.
They split their meager assets fair and square.
'Twas just about a conflict-free divorce
Except one issue made their tempers flare.

Another beating heart had come along.
Adored by both, each fought for custody.
The judge said, "Fighting over this is wrong"
And showed a plan on which they could agree.

So, now they share and keep a written log
To track the days that each has had the dog.

CHAPTER 19

The Morning After

THE MORNING AFTER

The morning after drinking too much beer,
A guy awoke, hung over on the floor.
"Oh, no!" he thought." I'm going to barf, I fear."
He wondered what he'd done the night before.

He went outside and couldn't find his car.
His wallet, keys, and phone were missing, too.
He prayed that they would still be at the bar,
Then vowed he'd quit. He'd drank his final brew.

Just then a friend showed up with all his stuff
And said, "You partied hard. Are you alright?"
Relieved, he answered, "Feelin' good enough.
How 'bout we all go out again tonight?"

His vow forgotten, he was heard to say,
"A good time's worth a lousy-feeling day."

NEW YEAR'S RESOLUTION

She woke up all hungover New Year's Day
And thought, "Things need to change. My life's a mess.
I can't believe how far I've gone astray."
There'd be a host of issues to address.

She ate too much and didn't exercise.
She drank a lot and smoked two packs a day.
She'd shared her bed with scores of scuzzy guys.
But life would change, beginning right away.

She'd failed at resolutions in the past.
And learned she shouldn't set her sights too high.
The cures for major problems never last,
So she'd select a lesser one to try.

She opted for a not-so-taxing chore.
She wouldn't fart in Walmart anymore.

BEER THERAPY

A guy whose self-esteem was very low
Woke up one day and thought, "I need a boost."
He'd heard about a place where he could go
Where higher self-esteem could be induced.

The sign out front read, "Welcome, glad you're here."
He entered and was greeted with a hug.
The place provided therapy through beer.
A therapist produced a frosty mug.

A few beers made him smarter than before.
His looks improved with each one he consumed.
The beer had caused his confidence to soar.
He felt invincible, but he was doomed.

His self-esteem fell back to low from high
When driving home he got a D.U.I.

TURNING OVER A NEW LEAF

A redneck felt the urge to change one day.
"My life," he mused, "need not be such a mess.
My vices must be getting in the way
And keeping me from finding happiness."

He told his pals, "I want a better life.
I plan to give up smoking, drinking beer,
Stop chasing women, get back with my wife,
And leave this bar and never come back here."

His buddies quickly came up with a scheme.
"Let's celebrate your better life!" they urged.
With booze and girls, they partied to extreme.
By morning, his intentions had been purged.

The will to change is not there anymore.
He's glad he learned what redneck friends are for.

ARTIFICIAL STUPIDITY

A software engineer was very bright.
In college he had gotten only A's.
Decisions made by him were always right,
Resulting in a lot of well-earned praise.

His reputation as an expert spread,
And when he put his talents on display,
His colleagues hung on every word he said.
But weekend nights he'd put his brain away.

He'd drink a lot but couldn't get enough,
Which led to saying things he should regret
And doing lots of really foolish stuff
His drunkenness would cause him to forget.

By Monday, he'd recover thoroughly
From alcohol induced stupidity.

CHAPTER 20

As Seen on TV

HURRICANE COVERAGE ON TV

Each time there was a major hurricane,
A TV weather guy was at the coast.
A lot of folks would say, "That guy's insane."
But taking risks was what he loved the most.

He always sought the most dramatic place
Where he could brace himself against the gale,
Where horizontal rain would pelt his face
And windblown objects threatened to impale.

But though his job was strictly to inform,
Distracted viewers focused more on him.
His deeds were more intriguing than the storm.
Alas, the guy had never learned to swim.

So, when a riptide swept him out to sea,
He nevermore was seen on live TV.

PET PEEVE

A lap dog's owner watched TV a lot.
So, he watched, too, while snuggling on her lap.
Some shows he liked, but others he did not,
And some he thought were positively crap.

If what his owner watched did not excite,
He'd either snooze or look the other way,
But one choice always caused him to alight
And do a deed to show her his dismay.

When pledge week rolled around on PBS,
She'd take him from the room and shut the door.
The interruptions caused him such distress
He'd show his ire by peeing on the floor.

Seems any time they air a decent show,
They interrupt it asking for your dough.

MIRACUFLEX, THE WONDER DRUG

Miracuflex, the drug for all your ills,
Cures common colds and flu in half a day,
Stops flatulence, bronchitis and the chills,
Treats Lyme disease, reverses tooth decay.

Miracuflex, the drug that guarantees
To shrink your tumors, hemorrhoids, and warts.
It cures arthritis, blindness, heart disease,
Obesity, and cancers of all sorts.

Stop taking it if you lose all your hair,
Turn blue, see spots, or you get short of breath.
If you collapse, and things turn dark, beware.
A very common side effect is death.

It's pricey though it could be almost free
If not for costly ads shown on TV.

INFOMERCIAL

He watched an infomercial on TV.
Restoring hair is what the product does.
He thought, "That guy once looked a lot like me,
A balding chap with just a bit of fuzz.

But now he's got a head that's full of hair,
It's long and wavy, thick and shiny black.
Admiring friends and neighbors stop and stare.
The infomercial product grew it back."

Convinced, he phoned and ordered right away.
The product came. He rubbed it on his head.
His teeth fell out, and he went blind that day.
He fainted, and the next day he was dead.

His corpse then sprouted splendid, flowing locks,
And folks said he looked great in his pine box.

CHAPTER 21

Taboo Topics, Politics, and Religion

TRUMP GOES TO HEAVEN

As Donald Trump approached the pearly gates,
A host of angels, dressed in riot gear
And serving as Saint Peter's delegates,
Informed him he would not be welcome here.

The leader said, "You see this massive wall?
We built it just to keep out folks like you.
St. Peter says you've got a lot of gall
To think there's any chance we'd let you through."

"C'mon," The Donald said. "Let's make a deal
Unless you want this tied up in the courts.
Just let me in. I'll make this place unreal.
I'll build hotels, casinos, and resorts."

The threat to sue caused laughter but no fear.
The angel said, "You'll find no lawyers here."

MOST DESPISED SPECIES

A rat and snake were talking in a bar.
Each claimed his species got the least respect.
The snake said, "We're despised the most by far."
The rat said, "Sorry, but that's not correct.

While squirrels and chipmunks both are rodents, too,
Folks think they're cute, but me, they try to kill."
The snake said," We help rid the world of you,
Yet people hate us, and they always will."

Then, both looked up and saw the bar's TV
Was showing a political debate,
And suddenly they found they could agree
That politicians garner far more hate.

Each raised a glass in toast, then quenched his thirst,
Both glad to know to know their species isn't worst.

SMOOTH TALKER

From when he learned to talk, all through his youth,
His way with words was talent rarely found.
He never lied but still could hide the truth
Or make the ordinary sound profound.

Small wonder he was always teacher's pet.
His pick-up lines bedazzled many a lass.
His calming voice and words could quell the threat
Of any bully who'd have kicked his ass.

He found his calling in the PR field.
A gifted wordsmith, skilled at twisting facts,
He mastered keeping lies and faults concealed
And verbally perfuming putrid acts.

His tale is like the typical ascent
Of White House spokesmen for the President.

ELECTION CAMPAIGN STRATEGIES

A man who ran for office made a vow.
He wouldn't bash the other candidate.
Civility is so uncommon now,
He hoped that voters might reward this trait.

Resisting great temptation to attack
The scumbag reputation of his foe,
He took the high road, always holding back,
And stuck to issues he thought apropos.

The other guy did not reciprocate.
He chose instead to slander, slam, and smear.
Though tactics such as these make some irate,
Election day made one thing very clear.

Despite the scumbag's sordid past and sins,
The low road through the gutter sadly wins.

PEARLY GATES

When at the pearly gates, he got upset.
He didn't know there'd be a lengthy line.
An usher angel told him, " Please don't fret.
Be patient and just try to act divine."

He saw a placard in the queue that read,
"Your wait time from this point is forty years."
"No way!" he thought, "I've got to move ahead,"
Then pushed his way in front of all his peers.

Saint Peter checked the date stamp on his wrist
And sternly said, "You're here before your time.
It's clear you've cut the line, and now I'm pissed,
Impatience in Eternity's a crime."

And then a trap door opened. Down he fell
And found no waiting at the gates of Hell.

CHAPTER 22

Misfits

A DOG EXPLAINS

I like to stop to smell the yellow snow.
I do a sniffing dance with dogs I meet.
My nose brings pleasures you will never know.
I roll in poop. It makes me smell so sweet.

I drink from the commode, then lick your face.
I leave my mark on hydrants, posts, and trees.
I go berserk when there's a squirrel to chase.
If these are faults, I beg forgiveness, please.

For I have traits that far outweigh these flaws.
I give my owner endless, perfect love.
I live to brighten days and that's because
I've come here as a gift from God above.

If humans all spread love and joy like me,
Oh, what a better place this world would be!

EARWORM

It started on a day at Disneyland.
At "It's A Small World" he first heard the tune,
And then a glitch that Disney hadn't planned
Confined him to the ride all afternoon.

It left an earworm planted in his brain
That haunted him for weeks, both night and day.
The song was slowly driving him insane.
He had to make the torture go away.

A Google Search and visit to a shrink
Both failed to make the torment disappear,
But then one night he had too much to drink,
And reasoned he'd hear less with one less ear.

Alas, this fix did not relieve his woe,
And now his friends have nicknamed him "Van Gogh."

LOVELY CALI

She never needed primping to look great.
She walked with a distinctive, regal prance.
With splendid, flaxen hair worn short and straight,
She often made heads turn to steal a glance.

Her huge brown eyes would telegraph her mood.
She almost always wore a happy smile.
Her lip would curl those rare times that she'd brood.
She lived epitomizing class and style.

But life was far from blissful at the start.
Her early days were absent love and care
Until a man who had a tender heart
Transformed her life and lifted her despair.

Delight and love both started to abound
The day Sam rescued Cali from the pound.

A GIRL NAMED SIRI

Her parents named her Siri years ago,
A very pretty, not so common name.
Back then there was no way that they could know
The iPhone lady would be named the same.

Folks thought that she should now know everything.
They sought directions, wanted her advice,
Asked private stuff, requested that she sing,
And many times were anything but nice.

She thought, " A name change might improve my life."
A lawyer filed the proper forms in court.
It seemed to put an end to all her strife.
Alas, her time of happiness was short.

Turns out her new name proved to be a curse.
She chose Alexa. Now, her life is worse.

ELMER FUDD RESEMBLANCE

A man who looked and talked like Elmer Fudd
Was lonely, sad, and yearned to find a mate,
But ladies seemed to think he was a dud.
At forty-two, he'd never had a date.

To fight despair, he came up with a plan.
He'd go to bars, the gym, and even church,
The places women go to find a man.
Alas, he turned up nothing from his search.

But then a kindly lady told him why.
"For starters, stalking rabbits is bizarre,
And no one wants a wimpy, bashful guy
Who's short and bald and can't pronounce an R.

The only hope for you is if you find
A rabbit-hating gal who's deaf and blind."

ROADKILL EULOGIES

A group of woodland creatures gathered by
A lifeless possum lying on the road.
They all took time to eulogize the guy,
Though few, if any, kudos were bestowed.

The skunk said, "He was smellier than me."
The squirrel claimed, "He tried to steal my nuts."
The deer remarked, "I think you'd all agree
He's dead cuz he was pokey and a klutz."

And on it went. They slammed him, one by one.
But then the possum moved. He wasn't dead.
Of course, this put an end to all their fun,
And all were quite embarrassed when he said,

"Just playin' possum. Wondered what you'd say
 If I had really bit the dust today."

ABOUT THE AUTHOR

Ken Mogren has been a nearly lifelong resident of Winona, MN, in the beautiful Mississippi River Valley. At Winona State University, he majored in Psychology and English and credits an understanding of human nature and good communication skills for success in a 43-year insurance industry career.

At about age 60, he rekindled a dormant interest in creative writing and began entering humorous sonnets in contests, enjoying a bit of success.

In retirement, he has picked up the pace, resulting in a collection of nearly 200 sonnets, with over 100 of these in this book, his first: Spunky Grandmas and Other Amusing Characters. Ken and his wife, Sally, enjoy traveling and spending time with their three sons and their families. He also serves as a volunteer on the non-profit boards of a hospital, university and theatre company. Ken's other interests include running, cycling, and cross-country skiing. He regularly competes in those sports and has won three national age group championships. He also enjoys kayaking and golf.

Other Humor & Wit Books
Or, Information Presented with a Smile
from MSI Press LLC

57 Steps to Paradise (P. Lorenz)

A Movie Lover's Search for Romance (J. Charnas)

Clean Your Plate! (Bayardelle)

Diary of an RVer during Quarantine (L. MacDonald)

Forget the Goal; the Journey Counts (A. Stites)

How My Cat Made Me a Better Man (J. Feig)

Mommy Poisoned Our House Guest (S. Leaver)

Of God, Rattlesnakes, and Okra (J. B. Easterling)

RV Oopsies (L. MacDonald)

Soccer Is Fun without Parents (P. Jonas)

The Musings of a Carolina Yankee (W. Amidon)

Travels with Elly (L. MacDonald)

Tucker & Me (A. Harvey)